TIME CHRONICLES

Mission
Victory

Written by Roderick Hunt
and illustrated by Alex Brychta

OXFORD

ABERDEENSHIRE LIBRARIES
WITHDRAWN FROM LIBRARY

4012228

Aberdeenshire Council Libraries	
4012228	
Askews & Holts	20-May-2019
JF	£7.75
J	AR RL3.8 PTS0.5

Before you begin …

Dear Reader,

Before you begin this Chronicle, you should know that Biff, Chip, Kipper and friends have become Time Runners. They are based in the Time Vault, a place that exists outside time. Their mission is to travel back in time to defeat the Virans.

Virans are dark energy in human form. Their aim is to destroy history and so bring chaos to the future.

The Time Runners have to be brave and self-reliant. They have a Zaptrap, which is a device to capture the Virans. They also have a Link, which is a bit like a mobile phone disguised as a yo-yo. The Link lets them communicate with the Time Vault. Apart from that, when on a mission, they are very much on their own!

Theodore Mortlock
Time Guardian

HMS Victory
Cape Trafalgar, 1805

HMS *Victory* is the Royal Navy's most famous warship, built between 1759 and 1765. She was Lord Nelson's flagship at the Battle of Trafalgar (1805). *Victory* has five decks and 104 cannons. At the Battle of Trafalgar, *Victory* carried over 7 tons of gunpowder.

Chapter 1

Tyler gazed at the TimeWeb. In the web of bright light, a dark patch had appeared. Slowly it began to pulsate.

"Virans!" he murmured. He pressed the alarm to call the others. At once they ran in from all over the Time Vault. First to arrive was Chip, followed by Wilf. The others were not far behind.

"What have we got?" called Biff, pulling her hair into a band as she came.

Tyler pulled his techno-chair closer to the TimeWeb and tapped the strange symbols on the keys of the Matrix.

"Date?" urged Wilma.

"Looks like 1805," muttered Tyler. He looked closely as a faint image began to form in the globe that glowed beside him. "It looks as if the Virans are interested in a ship. Yep! I've got it. HMS *Victory*."

"Nelson's flagship!" shouted Nadim. He clicked his fingers. "1805 was the Battle of Trafalgar. Wasn't that a sea battle? The Brits against the French and Spanish? The Virans couldn't do something to change the outcome of the battle, could they?"

"Who knows?" asked Neena. "If they could meddle with such an important event, think what it would do to unravel history."

"Who's going?" asked Wilma. "It has to be boys. Didn't they have boy sailors on warships in those days?"

Wilf looked at Chip. Chip nodded.

"We'll go," said Wilf, "but I've got a feeling this is going to be a tough mission."

They stepped into the portal together.

"I hope you aren't seasick," called Biff, but Tyler had already pressed the 'send' symbol on the Matrix.

Chip and Wilf had vanished.

Chapter 2

The first thing that Wilf noticed was the smell. It was of tar and an unpleasant smell like the stench of rotten eggs and mud.

In the dim light that seeped in down a flight of steps Wilf could see boxes, barrels, piles of canvas, stacks of wood, coils of heavy rope and bulging sacks. A rat ran out from behind a barrel and scuttled away.

Wilf was in a vast space that moved up and down. He could hear the creaking of timber and the sound of water slopping. Above he could hear shouting and the thud of heavy footsteps.

Wilf felt Chip's hand on his arm. "Chip!" he gasped nervously. "Thank goodness!"

"We must be in the hold on HMS *Victory*," said Chip.

At that moment, feet clattered down the steps. It was the ship's carpenter. He was wearing a leather apron and had wood shavings in his hair. The boys dived behind some boxes, but it was too late. They had been spotted.

"Stowaways!" the man bellowed. "Stowaways on board!"

He grabbed the boys and dragged them up the steps.

"We'll take you to the Bosun," he shouted. "You'll be punished for this, I've no doubt."

Chapter 3

Stowaways on board! The news spread like wildfire throughout the ship. Wilf and Chip were hauled up steep flights of steps from deck to deck. At last, they were dragged out into the sunshine of the quarterdeck.

Sailors stopped work and looked to see who the stowaways were. Some soldiers in red jackets gave a ragged cheer.

The Bosun was a large, rough-looking man with crooked teeth. He held a stiff rope, which he smacked against his hand.

"Who have we got 'ere?" he demanded. "Some small fish; tiddlers, I'd say!" He put his face close to Wilf's and yelled, "How did you get aboard, you young maggots?"

On the way up to the quarterdeck, Chip had stolen a look at his Link. Tyler had sent a download. Chip now stood to attention. "We are orphans, sir, but we are stout-hearted British lads. We want to serve our king and country with the bravest crew that ever sailed."

At this, some of the sailors gave a cheer.

"Quiet!" thundered the Bosun. "We beat stowaways with a cat o' nine tails, put them in irons and feed 'em bread and water. And that's what we'll do to you."

"I think not, Mr Bosun," a voice cut in. A man in full naval uniform had walked up quietly. He had heard what Chip said.

The Bosun saluted. "Begging your pardon, Captain Hardy, sir," he barked.

"I like spirit," the Captain said. "These boys have it. But they are lads, not men.

We don't flog children on my ship. Put them to work. Let them earn their keep. We'll send them back to Portsmouth as soon as we can."

"Aye, aye, sir!" snapped the Bosun. But when the captain had gone, he hissed, "You're lucky! But if you think it will be easy, think again!"

Chapter 4

Chip and Wilf were taken to the Purser and given a hammock and clothes called slops.

"Be sure to keep yer slops clean and yer 'ammock tidy," growled the Purser.

Tyler had sent more information.

DOWNLOAD FROM TYLER

820 men on ship. 21 are boy sailors. You are the youngest. You'll have hard dirty jobs. Just do them. Don't answer back.

Tyler was right about dirty jobs. Chip was
told to go and clean out the pens on the
upper gun deck where animals were kept.
Wilf was sent to scrub sails.

They were amazed how low and cramped
the decks were. Huge cannons held by heavy
ropes ran down the sides of each deck.

The men lived in small groups called a 'mess'. They ate and slept around the guns.

Chip and Wilf were put in a mess with six other boy sailors. The others were older, but one was a twelve year-old boy called Tom.

"You must be mad to stow away," sniffed Tom, whose nose was always running. He was carrying a barrel with rope handles. In it was a greasy stew of boiled mutton.

"Supper!" called Tom, slopping out the stew on to square wooden plates.

After the meal, a bell rang. "Bed time!" sniffed Tom. "Hang yer hammock on these hooks and get some shut-eye."

When they were in their hammocks, Wilf whispered, "How can we spot who might be a Viran? There are eight hundred men aboard and we don't go on certain decks."

Chip didn't answer. Despite the noise, the smells and his swaying hammock, he had fallen asleep.

Chapter 5

The next day was worse than the day before. Chip and Wilf had to scrub out wooden buckets. "I hate to think what they've been used for," said Chip.

DOWNLOAD FROM TYLER

You are powder monkeys. In battle, you run down to the ship's magazine on the orlop deck and carry gunpowder charges back to the gun crews.

But Tyler's information was wrong, for that afternoon Captain Hardy ordered the ship to go to battle stations.

"It's a drill," sniffed Tom. "The captain wants the guns fired and reloaded. So far, we ain't been quick enough."

The boys had been told to spread sand on the decks. "Stops us slipping," said Tom.

Chip remembered Tyler's download. "Do we run down to the magazine to get the gunpowder?" he asked.

"What!" scoffed Tom. "The ship has 104 guns. We'd never do it. And the charges are heavy. It's gunpowder, see, wrapped in paper – same size as the gun barrels. They put 'em in leather tubes. The tubes are passed from hand to hand in a human chain up to each deck. We run with them to the gun crews and bring back the empty ones."

A man walked by and both Chip and Wilf felt an icy chill. A shiver ran down Chip's spine. "Could this man be the Viran?" whispered Chip.

"If he is, what's he up to?" said Wilf.

The man spoke to an officer. "The Armourer has been taken ill, sir," the man said. "So I will be in charge of the gunpowder during the drill."

"Very good, Mr Scott," replied the officer. "Return to the magazine and I'll signal the drill to begin."

Tom grinned at Chip. "Put your hands over your ears when they fire the guns," he said.

Chapter 6

Chip sent a message to Tyler. All he had time to say was: "Viran – gunpowder," before the Bosun saw him and gave him a flick with his heavy rope.

"Get to your place," he roared. "And don't drop the charges."

Bells rang, whistles blew. A great shout went up: "Action stations!" Sailors ran to man the guns. More men rushed to form a line from the top of the ship to the bottom.

"Keep well to one side when you run with the charges," said Tom. "The guns roll backwards."

The order was given. "Fire!"

The noise was tremendous. The guns gave off thick clouds of white smoke. As each one was fired, the gun captains shouted at their crews, "Load with shot! Ram home!"

Chip and Wilf ran through the dense smoke with new charges.

Another order was given. "Stand down!" The drill was over.

"I'm glad about that," said Wilf. "I can't just smell the smoke, I can taste it.'"

Chapter 7

The decks returned to normal. The ship's boys were told to sweep up the sand. Every gun had been loaded and was now ready for battle when the time came.

The drill had gone well. For a reward, the men were given a ration of rum and water, called grog.

"God bless Lord Nelson," the men shouted as they drank the grog.

As Wilf swept near one of the guns he noticed the quill of a feather lying on the floor. It was filled with gunpowder. The gun captains pushed these into a narrow hole at the end of the cannon. A spark from a flint caused the gunpowder in the quill to flash. And this set off the huge charge in the barrel of the cannon.

"Boom!" said Wilf, as he showed the quill to Chip.

Chip's Link buzzed. It was Tyler.

DOWNLOAD FROM TYLER

Gunpowder is sulphur, saltpetre and charcoal. It's mixed on board. Viran mixes gunpowder with too much charcoal = weak gunpowder = battle lost!

Chip gasped. "Supposing all the cannons have been reloaded with dodgy gunpowder? Maybe Mr Scott, the Viran, made the Armourer ill so he could get to the powder."

Wilf held up the quill. "No one is going to believe us, Chip. To prove this we're going to have to fire a cannon ourselves. Tell Tyler to get ready. We may need a quick escape."

Chapter 8

Each day, the ship's boys were allowed up on the quarterdeck for a short time. Here were the smaller 12 pound cannons.

"We'll fire one of these," said Wilf. "We'll need to move fast. Make sure no one is nearby. Are you ready?"

Chip pulled the bung from the mouth of the cannon. Wilf took the breech-cover off and pushed the quill down.

"Cannon being fired," yelled Wilf. "Stand clear!" Then he pulled the cord.

The flintlock snapped down. There was a huge "boom" and a massive cloud of white smoke. The heavy gun shot backwards.

There were shouts as sailors and officers raced towards them. "Arrest those boys!"

"Watch the shot," Wilf yelled.

The cannon ball splashed into the sea about eighty metres from the ship.

"Mr Scott has ruined the gunpowder," shouted Chip. "The guns will be useless in battle."

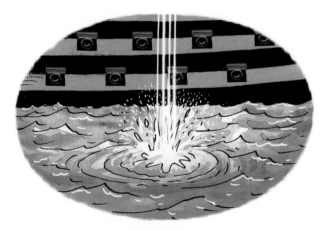

Chapter 9

"So what happened to the Viran?" asked Neena. "You didn't manage to zap him?"

Chip and Wilf were safely back in the Time Vault telling their story to the others. "No," said Wilf. "They thought he was a spy. He was arrested and put in irons. The Master Gunner fired a cannon from each deck. We were right. All the charges were useless."

"The Battle of Trafalgar could have been lost otherwise," said Wilma. "So you were heroes, then."

"No chance of that!" replied Chip. "We were arrested, too, for firing the cannon. The Bosun was ordered to beat us. Luckily, Tyler had the Portal ready for us to get away."

"Beaten, after what you did?" exclaimed Biff. "That's terrible!"

"No," sighed Wilf. "That was the British Navy for you. What's more, we never even got to see Lord Nelson."

Tyler's Mission Report

Location:	Date:
Cape Trafalgar	1805
Mission Status:	Viran Status:
Viran plot foiled.	1 arrested (not zapped!)

Notes:

It was tough for Chip and Wilf. Life on a warship in 1805 was hard, especially if you were a powder monkey (or boy Sailor Third Class). I'm amazed no one noticed Chip and Wilf had clean nails and smelled of soap and shampoo (in the Time Vault, they have a shower and put on clean clothes every day – well, most days, anyway!). Powder monkeys on the Victory had never had a bath (pongy!) So how did Wilf and Chip manage about using the loo? No soft toilet paper on ships in those days! The toilet was just a seat with a hole over the waves. Instead of toilet paper, you had to use the frayed end of a rope dangling in the sea!

Sign off: ....Tyler........................

History: downloaded!
Boy sailors on HMS *Victory*

HMS *Victory*

The youngest boy on board HMS *Victory* was a 12-year-old called Thomas Twitchett. Some boys were sent to sea as a punishment for crimes. Some went because they were orphans; others were sold into the Navy by their parents.